THE PSYCHOLOGY OF
MENTAL TOUGHNESS

A practical guide to developing mental toughness and overcoming life challenges

By

TRACY BRAVE

1

Table of contents
Introduction

- Strategic Guide to influence mental toughness

CHAPTER FOUR
How to Develop Mental Toughness: 14 Ways to Improve Your Mental Strength
- How to Develop a Robust Mental Attitude
- Building Resilience and Mental Toughness

CONCLUSION

Introduction

The proverb that "whatever doesn't kill you makes you stronger" is one that should be avoided since it is oversimplified, dishonest, and could have negative consequences. Even if it's true that some people who go through terrible experiences come out on the other side stronger, this is probably only the case for those people who were strong to begin with. Others are more likely to experience trauma as a result of horrific experiences, and their suffering may last for years or even decades afterwards.

The formation of a mentally tough mindset, a type of resilience that is a focused means to an end but does not contribute to the growth of a well-rounded, good mental and emotional life, can occur in persons who have endured a series of traumatic circumstances and come out on the other side. Lemn Sissay, a writer and poet, recently gave an interview to the BBC in which he discussed how, despite the fact that his upbringing helped him become more resilient, he would not wish the same level of fortitude on his worst enemy.

Since the 1960s, when the concept of mental or emotional resilience was initially investigated, it has been widely researched and is now well-established. But in today's world, the idea seems to have turned into a catch-all term for any and all problems that are related to stress and worry. In point of fact, it is a relatively passive idea that draws similarities from resilient engineering that is able to resist strong storms. It's a matter of "holding on" till the end.

On the other hand, the idea of mental toughness provides a single umbrella term that, while encompassing many of the key ideas relating to resilience, offers a more positive and targeted way of helping people deal with stressful situations. This is because the concept of mental toughness offers a more positive and targeted way of assisting people in dealing with stressful situations. The most important distinction is an emphasis placed not merely on hunkering down in the face of emotional storms but on the capacity to feel capable of actively seeking out tough environments and thriving within them. In this context, mental toughness refers to a positive psychological variable that is associated with achievement. It possesses psychologically beneficial properties that go beyond the ability to accept and cope with anxiety and include the ability to locate opportunities for personal development and advancement.

Mental Toughness (MT) is a feature that appears to be easily recognized by spectators, coaches, and players, but is significantly more elusive conceptually, being articulated differently in different settings (e.g., Crust, 2007; Gucciardi et al., 2015a) with no agreed-upon operational definition. Perhaps this is due to the fact that psychologically challenging activities are more readily apparent than the cognitions, attitudes, and emotions that accompany them. For instance, a person who perseveres and achieves their goals under circumstances in which they would typically be expected to stumble and fail would almost universally be labeled as exhibiting mentally tough behavior.

Despite the fact that MT is currently unconvincing as a fully defined psychological construct, there is unanimity over its nature. The majority of studies view MT as a rather stable disposition, albeit one that can alter in response to specific types of experience. Regarding MT, the adage "no pain, no gain" may be more than simple rhetoric. Several experts have identified the significance of adversity and hardship in the evolution of MT (Gucciardi, 2010). Current viewpoints show that MT represents a set of personal resources that are relevant for goal-directed conduct regardless of the degree of situational demands. In terms of MT development, research appears to confirm intuition and anecdotal evidence that athletes must be exposed to difficult settings, challenges, and adversity, rather than insulated from them.

Negative life events, crises, challenges, and stressful situations are often unavoidable and make up a big part of the human experience. For many people, adversity has negative effects on their physical and mental health, and these effects are often linked to problems with their social, educational, and occupational functioning.

Since some people seem to handle hard times better than others, researchers, policymakers, and the general public became interested in finding out what makes some people keep going when others give up.

Mental toughness (MT) has been studied as an important factor that makes people different and helps them deal with challenges and keep going when things get tough. MT is most well-known in sports, but its effects are now being seen in many other areas. It is a broad term for positive psychological resources that are important for success in many different situations.

Also, it shows not only a good way to deal with stress like rethinking stressful situations as chances to grow but also a high level of confidence in one's own abilities, which makes it possible to actively look for chances to grow as a person.

Intentionally left blank

CHAPTER ONE
Fundamental definition of Mental toughness and what it entails

The concept of "mental toughness" has been around for a very long time, although it is frequently misunderstood. Researchers have only recently started looking into this phenomenon, therefore we should count ourselves fortunate. Even though different researchers have arrived at different conclusions, it seems that mental toughness consists of four essential characteristics, namely motivation, the ability to remain focused despite distractions, confidence, and the capacity to deal with pressure. When thinking about how to develop mental toughness, one approach is to consider that it is sometimes taught, and other times it is caught. This can be a useful way to approach the development of mental toughness. Teaching mental toughness requires making a concerted effort to develop particular mental skills such as goal setting, relaxation, and concentration, although occasionally mental toughness is simply caught as a result of

being exposed to certain environmental factors e.g,
having a sibling who was older but pushed you to be
more competitive and to continually strive to
improve.

Mental toughness is a measure of an individual's
resilience and confidence, and it can be used to
predict success in a variety of arenas, including the
job, educational institutions, and athletic
competitions.

In the context of sports training, it emerged as a
general concept in the context of a set of attributes
that allow a person to become a better athlete and
are capable of coping with difficult training and
difficult competitive situations and emerging
without losing confidence. The context in which it
emerged as a general concept was sports training.

The phrase has been increasingly popular in the
coaching community, particularly among sport
psychologists, sports pundits, and business leaders
in recent decades.

To be successful in life, one must have a positive attitude and the mental fortitude to persevere through adversity. If a person wants to be successful in life, they must learn to remain composed even when faced with intense competition or demanding work conditions, for example.

When things get challenging, they need to keep a positive attitude and remember that if they put in enough effort, the outcome they want will most likely happen. If they can maintain a strong mental fortitude and persevere through the challenging times, they will be successful.

When things get tough, you have to keep grinding and do everything in your power to come back and win the game. This is something that particularly applies to the world of sports and athletes. An exceptional athlete must be able to handle pressure, have self-belief, and avoid lifestyle distractions in order to compete at their highest level.

It is easier to acquire this talent of mental toughness when one is still a youngster or when one is still a teenager. The earlier in life that one becomes psychologically tough, the more easily one would be able to handle the challenges of both athletics and life.

Mental toughness is a trait that is highly valued in athletic competition, but it is equally essential in many aspects of daily life.

When life gets challenging, one must acquire the ability to persevere in the face of adversity and resist the urge to feel sorry for themselves or give up.

They need to have the hunger for victory and the confidence that comes from knowing they can accomplish everything they set their minds to. This is the dividing line between good athletes and elite athletes (Jones et al.,2002).

The term "mental toughness" is widely used in colloquial speech to refer to any collection of positive traits that assists a person in coping with challenging circumstances.

The phrase "mental toughness" is frequently used in coaching and by sports commentators to refer to the mental state of players who are able to persevere through challenging sporting circumstances and ultimately achieve their goals. In support of this notion, a number of studies have found a correlation between mental toughness and achievements or successes in the sporting world.

On the other hand, it is frequently used as a shorthand explanation for any triumph at all, which is extremely problematic when used as an attribution. Numerous people have voiced their concerns about the usage of such a vague methodology.

However, within the past 15 years, scientific research has attempted to provide a formal definition of mental toughness as a psychological construct with clear measurement criteria. This paves the way for more robust analyses and comparisons to be made.

Because of its influence on performance, mental toughness has received a lot more attention during the past decade. Without having a strong mental game, an athlete will never reach their full potential in their performance.

In particular, three different research teams have come up with a definition for mental toughness as well as a construct definition for the term. The definition for mental toughness is the concept of being able to push past setbacks or barriers while maintaining a positive and competitive attitude.

This technique involves training the mind to be ready for these conditions and to be psychologically ready for whatever challenges are to come in one's life at any given point in time.

The Study Of The Psychology Behind Mental Strength

When people experience feelings of being overwhelmed, out of control, or unable to take constructive action, they frequently seek counseling. They may not be aware that counseling can actually make you stronger; they may have the misconception that they are coming to figure things out. Willpower alone is not enough to enable one to make decisions and stick with them.

How does this thing even function?

Unanticipated obstacles, such as a worldwide recession that forces otherwise successful businesses to close their doors, appear in our lives from time to time. When you find out that the company you've been working for for the past 20 years is going out of business the next week, this becomes your problem. Your entire universe has been turned upside down. You are unsure about what to do. You eventually get your breath, only to learn that you are confronted with scary alternatives. Are you planning to quit your job? Accept whatever career opportunity is presented to you? Should I renew my education by returning to school? Should we move into a smaller dwelling?

It's possible that you, along with a lot of other people, have a hard time picking up the phone to get things moving and putting the blame on yourself for being "weak" or "lazy." You just don't have the motivation to get it done no matter how hard you try. Perhaps you coerce yourself into doing action. Why was it still so difficult even then? Are you really that sluggish? And how do you get past that obstacle?

When the going gets tough, the tough get going.
When the going gets tough,
Being courageous in the face of hardship is a basic value in our culture. Because not everyone is capable of achieving it, it is considered to be an ideal. It is also much too simple to think about toughness under duress as a capability that one either possesses or does not possess.

However, there are not many absolutes in the world we live in. The majority of people are able to handle some situations successfully but struggle when confronted with others.

Is it possible for you to improve your ability to retain your cool under intense circumstances? Absolutely! Let's look at some ways you may strengthen your mind so that you can remain resilient in the face of challenges.

Think of an Olympic decathlete as someone who, over the course of two exhausting days, competes in ten different events that test their strength, skills, and endurance. The training of a decathlete must not disregard any of these qualities, and the competition

17

must be allowed sufficient time. In that case, they will be very good at the shot put event, but they won't even come close to winning the javelin throw or the 1500-meter race. To put it another way, if you want to strengthen your mental capabilities, you need to focus on improving both your strengths and your weaknesses.

A person who possesses mental toughness is one who is not afraid to confront obstacles head-on and is successful in finding solutions to those challenges. My point of view is that someone who is mentally tough has a mix of willpower, skill, and resilience. In what ways might treatment assist you in developing these qualities. Let's take a look at the components of mental toughness, as well as the ways in which psychotherapy addresses these aspects.

For instance, if you have a fear of driving over bridges, you might choose to avoid taking any route that requires you to cross a bridge.

To help you relax, your therapist may instruct you to take slow, deep belly breaths or demonstrate how to tighten and then release your muscles in order to bring about relaxation.

In addition to that, he might suggest that you try exposure treatment, which involves practicing relaxation breathing while gazing at the bridge from a distance.

After that, you might travel somewhere close to a real bridge and practice relaxation techniques there until you have calmed down sufficiently to be able to drive across the bridge.

Imagining the scenario from a greater distance at first, and then from a closer proximity as the exposure process progresses, can help you get ready for when you actually have to face it.

Skill

Awareness, critical thinking, and a broad viewpoint are the three components that comprise skill.

Attention and concentration are synonymous with awareness. These are established by conducting research into the problems that cause difficulty and

19

becoming aware of the factors that may contribute to those problems.

You may receive training in meditation to help you build your capacity to concentrate or consciously carry out day-to-day activities rather than bumbling your way through them in situations where life stress causes you to experience powerful emotions.

Keeping a journal, using diary cards, concentrating on your emotions until you develop a deeper intuition about what they're reflecting, and engaging in dreamwork are all additional methods that can be used to increase awareness. In dreamwork, your associations may provide insight into your mindset and the circumstances of your life.

Get advice and encouragement from people who know what it's like to deal with significant depression through private chat.

Sometimes brain dysfunctions that feel disabling, such as severe depression, bipolar disorder, or attention deficit hyperactivity disorder, can cause attention and focus to be compromised (ADHD).

Medication can be of particular assistance in the treatment of certain disorders. Substance misuse, which needs to be brought under control, can also lead to a reduction in one's level of awareness.

Escaping Avoidance

Some people find themselves stuck in a nuanced form of avoidance that gives the impression that they are doing something, but in reality, they are doing it in a dazed and half-hearted manner. For instance, a husband might ignore his wife's request to converse by going to his computer and surfing the Internet for several hours rather than responding to her request.

Or, a young woman loses herself in trashy novels but worries that she isn't making enough of an effort to get her life in order. This safe refuge might appear in a variety of ways. It isn't quite living, nor is it fully unconscious, and it gives the idea that you're doing something, but in reality, all it does is generate emptiness.

If you discover that you are in a state of lethargy, the first thing you should do is acknowledge that you are in this state. After that, stand up and engage in a different activity. Examine what you have been avoiding and, if possible, deal with it head-on; alternatively, if you are still experiencing roadblocks, investigate what you have been avoiding.

Thinking. Automatic thought recorders are one of the tools that cognitive therapists employ to assist patients in improving both their awareness and their thinking. The following is how they function:

There are some circumstances that put you off balance. As soon as you are able to, you should write down what occurred and investigate the thoughts that were prompted by the circumstance to determine whether or not those thoughts are an inaccurate depiction of what you saw.

After then, you evaluate the intensity of the sentiments that were triggered by those thoughts by writing them down and recording them.

The next step is to engage in a conversation with those thoughts in order to discover a more flexible response. In conclusion, you evaluate the degree of intensity of the feelings that are currently associated with that event.

Quite frequently, you will find that your emotional response has significantly mellowed, which will allow you to have a response that is more flexible moving forward.

You may experience some of the same benefits if, with the help of a therapist, you discuss similar circumstances, thoughts, feelings, and possible reactions.

She might also have you participate in role play as a means of bolstering your self-assurance and teaching you new abilities. All of these strategies help you think more clearly when you're under a lot of strain.

Dyslexia is an example of an inherited condition that can cause learning and attention issues for some people. Your therapist might send you to another professional for evaluation and include consideration of these concerns in your therapy plan.

Having perspective means being able to remove oneself from the present circumstance and examine it within its broader setting.

It's possible that a solution-focused therapist could assist you in visualizing the life you desire and getting started on the actions that will lead to that life.

You are encouraged to work with pictures that you generate on the spot when you participate in imaginative approaches like dreamwork, art therapy, or sand tray treatment.

You can realize, with the help of these approaches and others like them, that your unconscious mind already possesses the larger viewpoint that you are looking for.

Talk therapy is the strategy that is utilized most frequently to assist individuals in gaining perspective. Your therapist may direct you to investigate your current circumstance and the myriad of factors that have contributed to it.

Your behavior can be better understood by looking at it through the lens of unresolved conflicts from your childhood at times. This can help you make sense of responses that no longer make sense. Reading material that is assigned to you and a discussion of the findings of relevant research may also prove beneficial to your circumstances.

Resilience

To have staying power, you need to have resilience, which is a combination of things like patience, adaptability, self-care, and support from others.

Patience can help you avoid compounding problems and can make it possible for you to time your responses more effectively. Patience can also help you time your responses more effectively. It is taught through encouraging people to set objectives that are realistic.

If you practice meditation on a regular basis, you will develop the ability to maintain concentration in spite of distractions or discomfort, and you will be able to keep that focus for a longer period of time.

People who are so impatient that they frequently engage in rash, unplanned behavior may require training in emotion regulation and the ability to tolerate distress, or they may need to abstain from feeding addictions.

Anger is another emotion that might prompt rash actions to be taken. Classes on anger management and training to assert oneself in a manner that is more suitable and that takes into consideration the needs of others as well as one's own might be beneficial for people who are prone to rage.

Being willing to adjust one's course of action in response to shifting conditions is an essential component of flexibility. Getting more insight into your circumstance, including pondering the various options available to you, is the first step in the process. Dialog, role play, problem-solving, and communication skills training are some of the therapeutic methods that enhance flexibility.

Because the mind is connected to the body, it is necessary for people who are under stress to practice self-care. Having the stamina to deal with stress comes from being in good physical health. People frequently discover that they are able to begin to recover from depression after they begin engaging in regular exercise, consuming better meals, and discovering tried-and-true strategies to combat insomnia or seeking medical help if insomnia continues. People often stay in relationships or situations that are so stressful that they either need to find a solution to them or move on from them. A skilled therapist will be able to guide you through this process.

Compassion for oneself is an essential component of self-care, especially given the fact that very few people knowingly choose to remain stagnant in their lives. In most cases, they are doing the best that they can given the information and resources at their disposal. Your therapist will assist you in doing an audit of your self-care practices and will assist you in recognizing any medical conditions whose symptoms may be mistaken for those of a mental illness. A licensed therapist will be able to recognize the probability of this occurring and will know to recommend you for further medical evaluation. Resolving addictions that stand in the way of complete recovery is an essential part of practicing good self-care, just as is the case with growing other strengths.

Support is something that all of us require because we are more powerful as a group than as individuals. Creating a support network may require assistance in organizing and contacting the members of your family and community who are the most helpful to you. This assistance may come from your therapist as well as from other members of your treatment team.

Support groups and group therapy can be helpful for certain individuals. Also, if you are under a significant amount of stress or if your discovery process becomes so active that you could benefit from more time to digest your changes, your therapist may propose that you attend therapy sessions more frequently.

Towards a Change That Will Last

You have gained a better understanding of the qualities that contribute to mental toughness. You've also seen how your therapist can assist you in engaging in difficult work that contributes to the development of your specific strengths.

The development of a more optimistic outlook and the belief that one is capable of overcoming even the most challenging obstacles is one of the benefits that comes from a successful course of therapy. Developing a stronger mental fortitude is like getting a gift that keeps on giving throughout your entire life.

The Conceptualization of the Term Psychological Resilience

The ability to intellectually or emotionally deal with a catastrophe or to rapidly get back to where you were before the crisis is a key component of psychological resilience.

When a person makes use of "mental processes and behaviors in enhancing personal assets and shielding self from the possible negative impacts of stressors," they have demonstrated resilient behavior.

To put it another way, psychological resilience can be found in people who develop the psychological and behavioral capabilities that enable them to maintain composure in the face of chaos or emergency situations and to recover from traumatic experiences without suffering any long-term adverse effects.

The fact that it is difficult to assess and test this psychological construct due to the fact that resiliency can be construed in a multitude of ways gives rise to a significant amount of the criticism that is directed toward this subject.

The vast majority of psychological paradigms (biomedical, cognitive-behavioral, sociocultural, and so on) each have their own interpretation of what it means to be resilient, where it originates, and how it can be cultivated.

In spite of the fact that there are a plethora of definitions of psychological resilience, the majority of these definitions revolve around two key ideas: positive adaptation and adverse experiences.

Positive emotions, social support, and a person's natural toughness can all play a role in helping someone become more resilient, according to a large number of psychologists.

It is common practice to define resilience as a "positive adaptation" that occurs in response to a trying or difficult experience.

When a person is bombarded by daily stress," their "internal and external sense of equilibrium is upset, bringing challenges as well as opportunity.

On the other hand, the typical stresses of daily life can occasionally result in beneficial outcomes that build resilience. It is still not clear what the optimal degree of stress should be for each and every person.

Some people are better able to deal with higher levels of stress than others. Some psychologists are of the opinion that it is not the experience of stress itself that fosters resilience, but rather the individual's assessment of the stress they are undergoing and the level of control they believe they have over their lives.

People are able to practice this procedure since stress is present in their lives. According to Germain and Gitterman (1996), an individual is more likely to experience stress during times of difficult life transitions, such as those involving developmental and social change; traumatic life events, such as grief and loss; and environmental pressures, such as poverty and community violence.

A coherent sense of self that is able to maintain normative developmental tasks that occur at various stages of life is an essential component of resilience. Resilience can be defined as the integrated adaptation of physical, mental, and spiritual aspects in response to a given set of "good or bad" circumstances.

According to the Children's Institute at the University of Rochester, resilience research is focused on examining children who engage in life with optimism and humor despite devastating losses.

It is essential to keep in mind that exhibiting resilience involves more than simply surviving a very stressful experience; it also involves emerging from that experience with "competent functioning."

A person who possesses the trait of resilience is able to emerge from challenging situations stronger and better equipped than before.

A calm demeanor, high levels of self-esteem, the ability to plan ahead, and the presence of a supportive environment both within and beyond the family are all important components of psychological resilience.

Aaron Antonovsky claimed in 1979 that the likelihood of an individual having a resilient reaction to an event increases when the event is perceived as being understandable , managed, and meaningful in some way.

In its most prevalent form, the concept of psychological resilience is that of a process. It is something that may be utilized by an individual and is something that grows within an individual over time. Some people believe that it is a characteristic of the individual, which is a belief that is more well known as "resiliency."

According to the findings of the vast majority of recent studies, resilience is the quality that people possess when they are able to interact with the environments in which they live and take part in activities that either improve their well-being or shield them from the overpowering influence of risk factors.

The findings of this study could be used to bolster the argument that psychological resilience is more of a process than a feature. It is believed that resilience is something that can be developed. Making it a goal to work toward rather than a destination in and of itself.

Ray Williams, a successful Canadian entrepreneur and author, came to the conclusion that resilient people are those who are able to successfully navigate the challenges presented by their surroundings. He was of the opinion that there were essentially three ways that people could respond when confronted with a challenging circumstance.

Take a belligerent or combative stance in response. Turn off your brain because you're too overwhelmed.

Feel the emotion that is associated with the circumstance, then handle that feeling in an acceptable manner.

He believed that the third choice was the one that actually assists an individual in promoting their own wellness. People that exhibit resilience will behave in a manner consistent with this pattern. Their ability to adapt to challenging circumstances is the source of their resilience.

People who choose with the first or second choice are more likely to see themselves as helpless victims of their situation, or they may point the finger of blame at others for their predicament.

They are unable to adequately cope with their surroundings, which leads to them becoming reactive and having a tendency to cling to negative feelings. Because of this, it is frequently difficult to concentrate on finding solutions to problems or to recover.

Those that are more resilient will adapt to the challenges they face by adjusting their behavior, getting back up after falling, and searching for a way out. William believed that the development of resilience may be helped along by positive circumstances in addition to the ongoing use of coping strategies. These surroundings include social environments that are supportive, such as families, communities, and schools, and they also include social policies.

Intentionally left blank

CHAPTER TWO
The Science of Developing Mental Toughness in Your Health, Work, and Life

Have you ever pondered the factors that contribute to an individual's athletic ability? Or a good leader? Or an excellent parent? Why is it that some people are able to achieve their goals while others are not?

What exactly is the differentiating factor?

The majority of the time, we respond to inquiries like this by discussing the abilities of the best performers. It's safe to say that he's the most brilliant researcher in the lab. She is noticeably more nimble than the rest of the players on the team. He is extremely skilled in the art of corporate strategy.

However, I believe that we are all aware that there is more to the narrative than just that.

In point of fact, if you begin to investigate it, you'll find that your brains and talent don't play nearly as big of a role as you might initially believe they do. According to the studies that I have seen, intellect only accounts for thirty percent of your achievements, and that number is at the very upper end of the spectrum.

What has a more significant influence than either talent or intelligence? Strength of mind is required.

Research is beginning to show that your mental toughness, or "grit" as they call it, plays a more important role than anything else does in determining whether or not you are successful in achieving your goals in health, business, and life. This is true regardless of the field of study. This is encouraging news because, while you can't change much about the genes you were born with, you have a lot of control on how mentally resilient you become.

Why is it so vital to have a tough mental attitude? And what are some ways that you can improve it?

People who have strong mental fortitude make the decision from the very beginning of their lives that they will not let their circumstances define or ruin them. They are not the type of people who will roll into a ball and give up when things don't go their way.

They choose, rather, to pick themselves up, wipe away their tears, and view the obstacles as opportunities to demonstrate not just to themselves but also to the rest of the world that they are capable of overcoming anything and anything.

I'm happy to report some good news. The capacity for mental fortitude is not exclusive to superhumans. Instead, it is something that you can cultivate and become proficient in by practice and learning from your mistakes.

Take a moment to reflect on a time when you had to face adversity and emerge victorious. What personal qualities did you need to draw upon in order to get through that challenging period?

We don't give ourselves nearly enough credit for how far we've come or how much work it took to get to where we are now. Let's face it: life does not always cooperate with the plans you have made.

On the other hand, going through difficult experiences will make you a more powerful and resilient person. Those instances in my life that felt like they were collapsing, like a train wreck, turned out to be indicators that better things were actually coming back together again.

Let's discuss this topic right now.

The United States Military Academy at West Point welcomes a new class of cadets numbering around 1,300 individuals each and every year. Cadets are expected to perform exceptionally well on a battery of challenging examinations during the first summer after arriving on campus. Within the organization, this summer training camp is referred to as "Beast Barracks."

"Beast Barracks is purposely structured to push the very limits of cadets' physical, emotional, and cerebral capacities," are the comments of researchers who have studied West Point cadets.

You could be forgiven for assuming that the cadets who are able to successfully complete Beast Barracks are larger, more physically capable, or more intellectually capable than their contemporaries.

However, when Angela Duckworth, a researcher at the University of Pennsylvania, began following the cadets, she discovered something very different.

The topic of Duckworth's research is success, and more specifically, the ways in which mental fortitude, perseverance, and enthusiasm influence one's capacity to accomplish one's goals. She kept track of a total of 2,441 cadets at West Point, who were divided between two different entering classes. She took down each student's high school rank, SAT score, Leadership Potential Score. Which takes into account the amount of time spent on extracurricular activities. Physical Aptitude Exam score (which is a common test for measuring one's aptitude for physical activity), and Grit Scale score (which measures perseverance and passion for long–term goals).

What she discovered is as follows...

It was not a cadet's physical prowess, intellectual prowess, or capacity for leadership that accurately predicted whether or not they would graduate from Beast Barracks. Instead, it was the tenacity, perseverance, and drive to accomplish long-term objectives that proved to be the differentiating factor.

Cadets who scored one standard deviation or above on the Grit Scale were found to have a completion rate that was sixty percent greater than that of their classmates. It was not the cadet's natural ability, IQ, or genetics that foretold whether or not they would be successful; rather, it was their mental toughness.

When Is It Beneficial to Have a Tough Mental Attitude.

The research conducted by Duckworth has demonstrated the significance of mental toughness in a range of different domains.

In addition to the findings from the West Point study, she found that...

Undergraduate students in the Ivy League who exhibited greater grit also had higher grade point averages than their colleagues, despite the fact that they had lower SAT scores and were not as "clever." Instead of IQ, grit is a better indicator of which person will end up with a higher level of education when comparing two people of the same age who have different levels of schooling.

The participants in the National Spelling Bee outperform their contemporaries not because of their intelligence but because of their tenacity and their dedication to more continuous practice.
Additionally, mental fortitude and perseverance are beneficial in a variety of fields than education.
When Duckworth and her colleagues began interviewing great performers in a variety of fields, they heard stories that were strikingly similar...

Throughout the course of conducting interviews with professionals in a variety of fields, including investment banking, painting, journalism, academia, medicine, and the legal system, we developed the notion that grit is necessary for high accomplishment. When asked what characteristic distinguishes great performers in their respective fields, these individuals frequently indicated grit or a similar equivalent as being equally as important as brilliance. In point of fact, many people were impressed by the accomplishments of classmates who, at first glance, did not appear to have as much natural talent as others, but whose unwavering dedication to their goals was remarkable. Similarly, many people remarked with astonishment that exceptionally talented contemporaries did not achieve success at the highest levels of their profession.

Angela Duckworth

There is a good chance that you have witnessed evidence of this in your own experiences. Remember that one of your friends who completely wasted their abilities? What about the member of your team who has realized their full potential to the fullest extent possible? Have you ever known someone who was determined to achieve a goal, regardless of how long it took them to get there?

Your level of grit, mental toughness, and perseverance is the single most important characteristic that can predict your level of success in all aspects of your life, including your education, your work, and your health, more so than any other component that we can identify.

To put it another way, talent is significantly overrated.

Factors that contribute to a person's mental mental toughness

It's wonderful to have conversations on mental toughness, tenacity, and perseverance. However, what do all of those things look like when they are put into practice?

In a single phrase, tenacity and grit are synonymous with constancy.

Athletes that are mentally tougher tend to be more consistent than their peers. They never skip their exercise sessions. They never fail to turn in their homework. They can always count on the support of their teammates.

Leaders with strong mental fortitude are more reliable than their contemporaries. They are making progress toward a well-defined objective on a daily basis. They don't let things like short-term profitability, unfavorable criticism, or tight schedules stop them from moving forward in the direction of their vision. They make it a practice to bolster the capabilities of those in their immediate environment not just once, but repeatedly.

Artists, writers, and employees who are mentally tough tend to offer better results more consistently than their peers. They adhere to a timetable rather than only working whenever they feel inclined. They don't approach their work like amateurs, but rather like professionals. They start with the most vital task and don't avoid taking responsibility for anything.

The good news is that tenacity and determination may become your defining characteristics, even if you weren't blessed with a natural gift for anything. You can become more consistent. You have the ability to train yourself to have mental toughness that is beyond human.

In my experience, the real world is a good fit for these three different techniques...

1. Identify your own personal definition of mental toughness.
In order for the army cadets at West Point to prove that they were mentally tough, they had to complete the Beast Barracks for the full summer.

It's possible for you...

- Maintaining a perfect attendance record at the gym for a whole month
- Delivering your work two days in a row ahead of schedule.
- meditating every morning this week
- Doing one extra rep on each set at the gym today.

- Calling one friend to catch up every Saturday this month.
- Spending one hour doing something creative every evening this week.
- Going one week without eating processed or packaged food.
- Delivering your work two days in a row ahead of schedule, and so on.

Whatever it is, you need to have a firm grasp on what it is that you want. In the real world, mental toughness is related to tangible acts, even though it is a quality that exists in the abstract. You can't just become mentally tough; you have to demonstrate it to yourself by accomplishing something challenging in the actual world.

Which gets me to the second point I wanted to make...

2. Mental toughness can be built through a series of victories in less strenuous competitions.
A mind that is not strong cannot become dedicated to something nor can it be constant. How many times has your mind, rather than your body, informed you that you were exhausted, causing you

to skip a workout. How many repetitions have you skipped because your mind told you that you didn't need to do any more than nine. You shouldn't be concerned about the 10%." The majority of people, including myself, are probably in the thousands. And 99 percent of them are caused by mental flaws, not physical ones.

So frequently, we have the misconception that mental toughness refers to how we behave in challenging circumstances. What did you do in the game that decided who would win the championship? Is it possible for you to carry on with your life while grieving the loss of a member of your family? Have you been able to pull yourself back up following the failure of your business?

There is no question that extreme circumstances put our bravery, perseverance, and mental resilience to the test... But what about the typical situations that people face?

Mental fortitude can be compared to a muscle. In order for it to mature and advance, it requires effort. If you haven't challenged yourself in tens of thousands of different ways, it's only natural that you'll give up when the going gets truly tough.

However, this outcome is not inevitable at all.

Choose to complete the tenth repetition even though it would be simpler to just complete the nine repetitions. Make the conscious decision to create even when it would be simpler to consume. Pick the times to ask the follow-up question, even when accepting the offer would be simpler. Demonstrate to yourself, in a thousand little little ways, that you have the intestinal fortitude to get into the ring and wage a fight with life.

Mental fortitude can be developed by accumulating a series of smaller victories. Our "mental toughness muscle" is developed by the myriad of individual decisions that we deliberate about on a daily basis. We'd all like to have stronger minds, but you can't think your way to becoming mentally tough. Your mental toughness can be judged by how well you do in physical tasks.

3. Your routines, not your motivation, are the most important factor in determining your mental toughness.

Motivation might change at any moment. Willpower is a fluctuating quality.

To develop one's mental toughness, it is not necessary to amass an extraordinary amount of inspiration or bravery. It's about developing the routines that you do on a daily basis that make it possible for you to stay to a plan and prevail over obstacles and distractions over and over and over again.

People who are mentally strong do not necessarily need to be more daring, skilled, or intelligent; they only need to be more consistent. People who are mentally tough create strategies that assist them in maintaining concentration on the things that matter most to them, regardless of how many challenges life throws in their path. Their mental beliefs are built upon the foundation of their behaviors, which eventually differentiates them from other people.

The fundamental steps for forming a new habit are outlined here, along with links to additional information on how to carry out each phase.

- Establishing who you are is the first step.
- Keep your attention on the little things you do rather than the big changes you want to make.
- Create a routine that can be followed regardless of how motivated you are feeling at the time.
- Maintain your adherence to the plan, and pay no attention to the outcomes.

If you make a mistake, you need to get back on track as soon as you possibly can.

Your routines are the foundation of your mental fortitude. The key is to be more consistent in carrying out the tasks that you are already aware you should be performing. It comes down to how committed you are to engaging in regular practice and how well you can keep to a routine.

How did you go about building up your mental Toughness.

Our goal as a community is crystal clear: we want to live happy, healthy lives while also making a positive impact on the rest of the world.

To this end, I consider it my duty to provide you with the most up-to-date knowledge, ideas, and methods that will enable you to lead a healthier lifestyle, achieve greater levels of happiness, and have a more significant effect in both your personal and professional endeavors.

But regardless of the plans we talk about, the objectives we strive for, or the future we imagine for ourselves and the people around us, the fact remains that. Without mental fortitude, determination, and tenacity, none of it will be able to materialize into reality.

The majority of people, when faced with challenging circumstances, look for something simpler to focus their efforts on. People that are psychologically tough find a way to keep moving forward even when things become challenging for them.

There are always going to be trying circumstances that call for extraordinary displays of bravery, tenacity, and determination.Toughness, on the other hand, can be reduced to a matter of being more consistent than the majority of individuals in almost all aspects of one's life.

Psychological practices geared toward the development of mental toughness

Mental toughness has been identified by specialists as one of the most important factors that can be used to predict success in high-pressure circumstances. When you are up against adversity, having mental toughness can assist you in maintaining high levels of performance, efficiently coping with the situation, and keeping control. But what happens if mental toughness isn't your normal, default state of mind? Is it possible for you to attain your goals despite the continual stress in your life?

Researchers were prompted as a result to consider whether or not mental toughness is a skill that can be trained. They developed the hypothesis that certain psychological tactics targeted at increasing resilience are useful for helping people perform effectively under pressure and found support for their hypothesis.

Developing one's mental fortitude in challenging circumstances
It is not an easy chore to work under settings that are difficult on a daily basis. You are supposed to be quick, efficient, and to do better than the other people in your field. It is easy to comprehend how a person may go from being an industry leader to experiencing feelings of being overworked, weary, and on the verge of burnout in their job.

Having said that, there are some individuals who are in a position to withstand the onslaught of ever-increasing pressures. They are aware that even while there may not be much that they can do to change the environment, they can modify how they react to the stress that is present in their lives. This encapsulates the dual nature of stress, which consists of the external demands that are imposed by the situation as well as the individual's internal response to react accordingly. People who have a higher mental toughness are more likely to concentrate on the malleability of their own internal response and the aspects of it that they have control over.

According to the findings of certain studies, mental toughness can be characterized by qualities such as determination, focus, confidence, perseverance, a good attitude, the ability to regulate emotions, and a desire to be successful. It divides individuals who are able to thrive off of pressure from others who buckle under it in many different ways.

Methods for developing mental toughness

You can build up your mental toughness and increase your resilience to the effects of stress by putting the following strategies into practice.

Take charge of your level of arousal.
There is a sweet spot of emotional arousal that allows for optimum performance, in accordance with the well-known Yerkes-Dodson law. If we are not sufficiently aroused, or if we are overly stimulated, our performance will begin to suffer.

You, too, would like the level to be "just right," like Goldilocks did.

The first thing you need to do is determine which side of the curve you are currently on. Do you feel like you have the right amount of anxiety, or do you feel like you have too much?
The subsequent action is to make modifications. If your level of arousal is too high and you need to bring it down, strategy 1 is what you should do.

If your level of arousal is too low and you need to ramp it up, method 2 is a good option for you. After you've been using these strategies for a while, it's a good idea to calibrate and check in with yourself to ensure that you're still operating within the optimal range.

Progressive Muscle Relaxation (PMR) is a technique that enables you to cope with high levels of stress and anxiety.

Tactic 1 is to "turn it down," which stands for "progressive muscle relaxation." According to a number of studies, frequent practice of PMR can alleviate test-related anxiety, as well as regulate mood, manage insomnia, and combat cancer-related symptoms.

To begin, go into a seated or lying down position and perform this procedure. The next step is to inhale while simultaneously flexing a particular muscle, for example, your calf, for a whole six seconds. After that, you should quickly let go of the tension in that muscle.

After you've rested for ten seconds, proceed to the next muscle group.

Focus your attention on the sensation that occurs in your muscles as they ease off of their contracted state. Imagine that the things that cause you stress in your life are melting away as you let go of the tension in your body.

Carry on in this manner for the next ten to twenty minutes, moving slowly up your body from your toes to your nose as you go.

The second strategy, known as "turning it up," is to engage in some form of physical activity. This is one of the most effective ways to increase your level of arousal. Your muscles put in extra time and effort whenever you engage in physical activity.

This indicates that they are emitting more carbon dioxide and consuming a greater quantity of oxygen than they typically would. The rate at which you breathe quickens, and your circulatory system begins to work harder, so that you can make up for the lack of oxygen. The combination of these factors will put you in a state of heightened arousal.

Without having to leave your desk, you can perform any of the following activities to get a good workout without having to go to the gym:

Squat in a chair Position your feet so that they are hip-width apart and point the tips of your toes slightly outward. After that, go into a seated position by bending your knees and squatting down as if you were sitting in a chair.

Tricep Dips: While seated, position your hands so that they are slightly wider than your shoulders and rest them on the edge of your seat.

 The next step is to slide your body off the seat, and lower yourself to the ground while maintaining the same posture for your hands.

The next step is to elevate your body by utilizing your arms. You have the option of either bending or keeping your knees straight. Continue doing this for the next five minutes.

Carry on conversations with yourself, but keep a safe distance from anything critical.
Keeping a positive frame of mind can be challenging. After all, there is a natural tendency within the mind to focus on the negative. However, a number of studies have demonstrated that a person can improve their performance by having a positive internal dialogue with themselves.

In order to gain the benefits of positive self-talk, try your hand at the following steps:

Picture yourself in a predicament where you could benefit from some words of encouragement.

Put in writing a few things that you would say to yourself.
You should substitute a pronoun for the third person for every first person pronoun that you have written down.

Make one or more of these sayings your new mantra and repeat them to yourself whenever you feel like you need a boost of confidence.

According to the findings of a study conducted at the University of Michigan, employing first-person pronouns such as "I," "we," and "us", may make it more difficult for a person to engage in goal-directed behavior. Individuals who refrain from using first-person pronouns in self-talk express less discomfort, engage in less maladaptive post-event processing, and regard stress as a challenge rather than a danger, according to the findings of a series of experiments conducted by academics.

positive self talk

An additional useful strategy is to address yourself in the third person. Research in this area has demonstrated that doing so makes it easier to regulate one's emotions and increases one's level of self-control. It is as easy as writing down your typical self-talk and then replacing all of the personal pronouns with your own name, as if someone else were talking about you. This will give the impression that you are being spoken about by another person. It helps to inject some psychological distance into a situation, which enables you to relate to the stress in a way that feels less personal. This allows you to deal with the situation more effectively.

Set productive goals for yourself and work hard to achieve them.
Being too optimistic about one's ability to achieve one's goals might be counterproductive to that goal's actual accomplishment.

Once you've decided on a certain objective, the most important thing you can do is to refrain from daydreaming about obtaining it.

A study conducted at the University of Hamburg found that when individuals were overly enthusiastic about their chances of achieving their goals, the study found that those people had a lower chance of really accomplishing their goals.

The act of thinking positively might deceive your mind into believing that you have already achieved your objective. This triggers a physiological response, which enables you to relax and puts you in a state of complacency, both of which are beneficial effects. In other words, the uplifting sensation of goal optimism will lead you to believe that you are nearer to the desired conclusion than is actually the case.

The following are some pointers to keep your optimism bias in control and to keep you working hard toward your goal:

Be honest with yourself about the gap between where you are now and where you want to be, and practice visualizing that gap between the actual vs. the ideal. You should aim for something that is extremely difficult to achieve and very far in the future.

You can test whether or not you have an optimistic bias by first asking yourself how probable it is that you will reach that goal, and then cross-checking that answer by inquiring of others about the likelihood that they believe you will achieve the goal. Is there a disparity between the two? If you answered "yes," then it appears that you have some work ahead of you.

Recap on the benefits of mental toughness

When you are placed in a stressful atmosphere, you have two choices: you may either give in to the pressure and allow yourself to be overcome by it, or you can be resilient and rise above the challenges you face. According to the findings of this study, tenacity and mental strength are prerequisites for long-term success. Mental toughness is necessary to help you achieve your goals in the face of failure and unrelenting hardship, and it is essential whether you are joining the military or doing your work duties on a day-to-day basis.

CHAPTER THREE
Mental toughness and resilience development

To begin, having mental toughness has nothing to do with being macho in any meaning of the word. Everything hinges on our capability of becoming "the best version of ourselves that we can be at any given moment." Obviously, this is one of the most important aspects of development work for almost everyone on the entire planet.

It is a psychological theory that is supported by a lot of research. A person's level of mental toughness is a factor that plays a big role in determining how they react to the various stresses, pressures, opportunities, and challenges that life throws at them. Its origins can be traced back to Health Psychology.

It plays a significant part in gaining an understanding of wellbeing. The notion of "mental toughness" was first introduced in the field of sports psychology, where it has since become an integral part of the analysis of performance.

Because it explains "how we think," mental toughness is distinct from the vast majority of personality traits that are commonly utilized. The majority of the personality models and assessments that are used in the process of developing people and organizations focus on characterizing and predicting behavior, or "what we do when we are presented with situations." Having this knowledge is helpful, without a doubt, but it may not be as beneficial as figuring out "why we act the way we do."

The opportunity to gain such a perspective can be gained through an understanding of mental toughness. This is of the utmost significance if we are to alter behavior when it is necessary to do so and if we are to comprehend the reasons why certain occurrences cause problems for some people but not for others.

The person who developed the 4Cs framework, which is now the most widely adopted in the world, Professor Peter Clough, describes it as "the mindset to deal with life as it happens, taking setbacks in our stride, and understanding that we will experience life's ups and downs but that we can also see opportunity even in the dark times." This is a useful description of the framework.

According to research, mental toughness has a strong correlation with performance, wellbeing, mental agility, and aspirations, all of which are interrelated and all of which are essential to the achievement of success for both individuals and organizations.

There is also a range encompassing mental toughness. On one extreme of the spectrum, we have mental toughness, and on the other, mental sensitivity.
These are not means to categorize people, nor are they indicators of right and wrong. Both extremes have the potential to be both strong and weak in their own ways. We all exist at different points along the range.

If someone is self-aware about their mental toughness and develops ways to put what they learn into practice, it is entirely feasible for a psychologically sensitive person to be productive and successful. The same can be said for people who are mentally resilient. They do not have the same level of self-awareness, which can cause them to suffer.

The mindset that every individual adopts in all that they do is referred to as mental toughness, and it is critically necessary and helpful for everyone on two levels.

To begin, it clarifies the reasons for individuals' and organizations' patterns of behavior. Personality can be defined as an individual's characteristic pattern of thinking, feeling, and acting, and the personality of an individual can explain individual differences as well as how individuals behave in particular circumstances.

A person's mindset can be described by the personality trait known as "mental toughness." In order to understand why people behave in a certain way, it investigates the thoughts and feelings that are going through an individual's head. Therefore, there is an undeniable connection between attitudes and actions.

Mindset can be thought of as both a precursor to behavior and an explanation for much of that behavior. One way to think of mindset is like this:

Second, research and case studies conducted all over the world have shown that mental toughness is a major role in the majority of the outcomes that are considered to be important for both individuals and organizations, including the following:

Performance: being able to explain up to a quarter of the difference in overall performance between persons
People that are mentally tough accomplish more, work with greater purpose, have a higher dedication to the cause they are working for, and are more competitive. This results in improved output, delivery that is both on time and on goal, as well as improved attendance.

- Happier individuals who are in good health. People who are mentally tough are better able to cope with stress, have better attendance, are less likely to develop mental health problems, sleep better, and are less vulnerable to being bullied. They can remain cool and collected under duress.

- Positive Behaviour
increased engagement in activities.
People who have developed their mental toughness are more optimistic, have a greater sense of "can do," react positively to change and adversity, demonstrate improved attendance, are more inclined to contribute to a positive culture, take on new challenges, and volunteer for new chances and activities.

- More of a goal-oriented outlook on learning openness.
People that are mentally tough have higher aspirations and are willing to take on greater levels of danger.

There are several advantages that come with having a strong mental toughness, both for individuals and for organizations. The results of research carried out all over the world have led researchers to the conclusion that persons with greater levels of mental toughness, as measured by the MTQ48, have the following benefits:

Improved performance; it accounts for as much as a quarter of the variation in overall workplace performance.
Increased positivism and the adoption of a more "can do" attitude, which results in improved rapport and connectivity with coworkers.
A higher level of wellbeing, including increased contentment and improved stress control.
Change management can be defined as a response to organizational change that is more relaxed and causes less stress.
Increased aspirations refer to having a higher level of ambition, as well as confidence in one's ability to accomplish one's goals and a greater determination to persist in order to do so.

Because of these factors, mental toughness is of utmost importance for an individual as well as an organization, particularly during times of significant change. Mental toughness is an essential quality for leaders, people who aspire to be leaders, those who work in vocations that are demanding and unforgiving, or who operate in conditions that involve uncertainty or dynamic change.

Organizations, regardless of whether they operate in the education, health, government, corporate, or public sectors, need to be able to adapt to change, have a mindset that is set up for it, and be resilient.

Strategies for Enhancing Your Mental Strength

The more your mental power, the better equipped you will be to overcome life's obstacles.

Most people understand how to develop physical strength, but there is a great deal of confusion about how to create mental strength. Although there are several activities that might help you become mentally strong, the following three are the most effective:

- Talk to yourself as though you were a trusted friend.

The Laboratory of Neuro Imaging estimates that humans have approximately 70,000 thoughts every day. That implies you have 70,000 chances to either strengthen yourself or weaken yourself.

Your thoughts have a significant impact on your emotions and actions. In actuality, your inner monologue often becomes a self-fulfilling prophecy. Thoughts such as "I will never be hired for this job" or "No one ever listens to me" might influence one's conduct in a way that brings about the predicted outcomes.

Replace excessively negative beliefs with more realistic ones through practice. Remind yourself that your negative ideas, such as "I'm a loser and I'll never amount to anything," are not always accurate.

Think about "What would I say to a friend who said this about herself?" After that, speak these kind words to yourself.

- Take responsibility for your feelings.

Your mental strength will diminish if you permit your emotions to govern your life. There is nothing wrong with occasionally being in a poor mood, but remaining in a negative state can be dangerous. If you're not careful, sadness can lead to self-pity, anger to bitterness, and mild anxiety to paralyzing fear.

Many issues are caused by the desire to avoid suffering. Those who dread failure, for instance, frequently avoid new difficulties in an effort to control their anxiety. Avoiding emotional discomfort, however, is typically a short-term solution that leads to long-term issues.

Develop an understanding of the impact your emotions have on your life. Determine that you will be in charge of your emotions, so that they do not control you. Take command of your life by addressing unpleasant emotions head-on. The more you practice tolerating discomfort, the greater your confidence in your ability to embrace new challenges will grow.

- Be productive regardless of the conditions.

It is impossible to have mental fortitude when engaged in self-destructive habits that undermine your best efforts. Yet, the majority of individuals engage in several counterproductive behaviors on a regular basis.

Many of these unhealthy behaviors, such as complaining about your boss, throwing a pity party for yourself, or attempting to please everyone, may appear harmless, but they may wreak havoc on your mental health. When you combine these negative behaviors with your positive ones, your efforts become counterproductive.

You have limited time and energy in this lifetime. Spending your time and energy on activities that mentally robust people avoid will exhaust you and hinder your progress toward your goals.

Develop mental fortitude

Everyone has the capacity to develop mental resilience. Developing mental muscle, like gaining physical strength, involves focus and effort. The more you practice, the greater your capacity to manage your thoughts, control your emotions, and behave successfully regardless of your surroundings.

Learning how to exercise your mind is the key to realizing your full potential in life. Whether your goal is to become an excellent athlete or a more patient parent, mental strength will assist you in achieving your objectives.

- Cultivate an Unshakeable Sense of Confidence

Nobody is born with an unwavering sense of self-assurance. Everyone you've met who possesses this quality does so as a result of putting in a lot of hard work to cultivate it. This is why they have it.

In the words of Maxwell Maltz from the past:

"Driving through life with your hand brake on because you don't respect yourself is like a joke,"

Strength of mind is what enables a person to absorb blows and continue moving forward, allowing them to avoid succumbing to defeat despite physical wounds sustained in the process.

The muscles of one's self-assurance can be strengthened by anyone. The question that has to be answered is how one may practice being confident when one does not feel as though they have something to be confident about.

Having a prosperous life is entirely dependent on one cultivating and conditioning positive fundamental beliefs on a daily basis. Because of this, I am a major believer in the effectiveness of regularly repeated positive affirmations to oneself.

You have to have faith that you are superior to your limiting beliefs in order to go forward. When in doubt, put on an act until you feel the real thing. After you have convinced yourself that you are wonderful and have the ability to accomplish anything, you will automatically begin to live the sensation that you have.

- Acknowledge that you are Responsible for Your Own Life

It is easy to place responsibility for one's issues on the outside world when one feels as though the world is closing in on them. Having this mentality, however, will only serve to make you feel more powerless.

If you are consistently saying to yourself, "Bad things always happen to me," then life will feel like a perpetual battle for you. Be mindful of the words you choose to utter, for the universe is always listening.

You can't sit around and hope that someone will come along and improve your life for you. If you are serious in assisting oneself, it is imperative that you do this. You have the ability to take charge of your own life and be responsible for its outcomes.

There is no hope in achieving any of your goals or dreams. You will begin to step into your power as soon as you acknowledge and begin to actively live in accordance with that fact.

- Recast Obstacles as Opportunities for Personal Development

Failures are neither fatal nor irreversible. In point of fact, there are periods of time when it is really important to be knocked down by life.

There are times when you have to reach your emotional breaking point or your rock bottom before you are finally ready to make a change in your life. If you now believe that you have reached rock bottom, the good news is that there is nowhere else for you to go but up from here. The only path forward is upward!

My experience has taught me that falling to one's lowest point can serve as both a spur for personal growth and the basis upon which one can construct a new life for oneself.

I like to think of failures and obstacles as signposts that are there to shock me awake and bring me back to reality. When I find myself in a rut, it's usually because I've allowed myself to become overly accustomed to my surroundings or because I haven't been paying attention to my gut instincts.

It is up to you to view setbacks as excellent opportunities to reroute and refocus your life, but such opportunities are there for the taking. I want to urge you to think of the difficulties you are facing as chances for personal development.

The next time it seems like nothing is going your way, take a step back and ask yourself what the challenge is teaching you. Stepping back will give you perspective. Your mental well-being should absolutely be at the top of your priority list.

There is a silver lining to every cloud. You will be better equipped to look any future obstacle dead in the eye and wink at it if you learn how to accept the challenges you are currently facing and learn how to embrace them.

- Have Command of Your Emotions

How do you handle it when everything goes to pieces? Do you allow yourself to become overwhelmed and lose control, or do you take a step back, assess the situation, and then take appropriate action.

It's not always possible to exert control over how you feel. The only thing you have any control over is how you react to the feelings you are experiencing.

You might be able to have some effect on the final result, but everything else is completely out of your control. If you don't learn to control your feelings, your feelings will wind up controlling you, and if that happens, it will be very difficult for you to help yourself.

The concept presented in "The Secret Life of the Brain," according to which we have some degree of control over our emotional responses. Instead, we create our feelings by drawing conclusions about the future based on the information we gleaned from the past.

This line of thinking lends credence to the idea that you are the one who creates the reality you experience. This indicates that you are, and will continue to be, in command of your life as well as your feelings at all times.

Having a more conscious approach to your daily activities is the most effective strategy for gaining more command over the emotional responses you experience. Being present and having a greater awareness of oneself, one's experiences, and one's role in relation to those experiences are essential to addressing this issue.

If you feel yourself becoming overwhelmed in the future, remember to take a few deep breaths and focus on calming down your emotional core. Give yourself the time and space you need to decide how you will react to the situation.

Meditation May Change Your Life: The Power of Mindfulness is a resource where you can gain additional knowledge regarding the practice of mindfulness.

- Force Yourself to Get Out of Your Comfort Zone

In my opinion, progress can never be achieved at the expense of comfort. Your comfort zone may seem like a good location to hang out, but the truth is that there is no room for growth there.

According to the findings of recent research conducted at Yale University, uncertainty triggers the brain to transmit a signal that begins the process of learning. This suggests that putting yourself in precarious situations that make you feel uneasy is essential to your capacity for personal development and professional achievement.

You can help yourself by putting yourself in uncomfortable situations.
Do you believe that some of the most successful people in the world got to where they are now by sipping apple martinis and lazing around on beaches. Never in a million years.

They put in an incredible amount of effort and took on a lot of danger in order to make their ambitions come true. In a nutshell, in spite of their concerns, they decided to take significant action.

I propose that you set a goal for yourself to accomplish one thing every day that challenges your brain capacity. This is how you get behind the wheel of your own life and take control of it.

Do you still find yourself pondering the best way to move beyond your safety zone? It is highly recommended that you read the book in question.

Strategic Guide to influence mental toughness

1. Emotional intelligence.

2. Confidence.

3.The capacity to neutralize poisonous individuals.

4. Being able to

There are times in our lives when our mental fortitude is put to the test. It could be due to a poisonous friend or coworker, a dead-end job, or a troubled relationship.

Regardless of the difficulty, you must be courageous, adopt a fresh perspective, and act decisively if you want to overcome it.

It sounds simple. Everyone wants nice friends, employment, and relationships.

But it's not.

Being psychologically strong is difficult, especially when you feel stuck. Only the most mentally robust individuals possess the fortitude, audacity, and tenacity necessary to defy convention and strike out in a brave new direction.

It is remarkable how psychologically tough individuals distinguish themselves from the pack. Where others perceive insurmountable obstacles, they see obstacles to conquer.

When Thomas Edison's factory burned down in 1914, destroying unique prototypes and inflicting $23 million in damages, Edison's response was straightforward: "Thankfully, all of our errors were destroyed. Now we can begin over from scratch."

Edison's response exemplifies mental fortitude by recognizing opportunity and taking action in the face of adversity.

There are behaviors that can be formed to enhance mental toughness. In truth, the characteristics of psychologically tough people are methods that you may implement immediately.

Emotional intelligence is the foundation of psychological resilience. You cannot be mentally tough if you cannot fully comprehend and accept intensely negative emotions, as well as accomplish something constructive with them. Moments that challenge your mental toughness ultimately evaluate your emotional IQ (EQ).

In contrast to your fixed IQ, your EQ is a malleable skill that may be enhanced through understanding and effort. It's no surprise that 90% of top achievers have high EQs and that those with high EQs earn (on average) $28,000 more per year than those with low EQs.

Unfortunately, EQ abilities are scarce. Only 36% of the over a million individuals evaluated by TalentSmart can reliably identify their emotions in real time.

"Whether you believe you can or believe you cannot, you are correct." Henry Ford

Mentally tough individuals agree with Ford's assertion that your mindset has a significant impact on your success. This is not merely a motivational tool; it is a fact.

A recent study conducted at the University of Melbourne revealed that confident individuals earned better earnings and were promoted more rapidly than others.

True confidence, as opposed to the false confidence people portray to hide their fears, has a distinct appearance. Mentally tough people have an advantage over those who are uncertain and fearful because their confidence inspires others and helps them get things done.

Dealing with problematic people is irritating and tiring for the majority of people. Mentally robust individuals manage their relationships with toxic individuals by keeping their emotions in check. When confronting a poisonous individual, they tackle the situation rationally. They are able to recognise their emotions and refrain from allowing anger or irritation to feed the pandemonium. They also examine the perspective of the difficult individual and are able to identify common ground and solutions to issues. Even when everything goes awry, mentally strong people are able to take the poisonous person with a grain of salt in order to avoid being brought down by them.

Mentally tough individuals are adaptable and adaptive. They are aware that the fear of change is debilitating and poses a significant threat to their prosperity and pleasure. They anticipate impending change and formulate a plan of action in the event that it occurs.

Only when you accept change can you see its benefits. You must have an open mind and open arms in order to perceive and take advantage of the opportunities that change presents.

Continue doing the same things you've always done in the vain notion that ignoring change would make it disappear. Ultimately, the definition of insanity is doing something repeatedly and expecting a different outcome.

University of California, San Francisco research has shown that the more difficult it is for you to say no, the more likely you are to experience stress, burnout, and even despair. Mentally tough individuals are aware that saying no is beneficial, and they have the self-respect and foresight to make a clear refusal.

When it's time to say no, mentally strong individuals avoid statements such as "I don't think I can" and "I'm not sure." They confidently decline additional commitments because they recognize that doing so fulfills their present obligations and affords them the opportunity to successfully complete them.

Mentally tough individuals are also capable of exercising self-control by saying no to oneself. They defer satisfaction and prevent harmful impulsive actions.

Mentally tough individuals are aware that, when all is said and done, they will regret their missed opportunities far more than their failures. Don't be frightened to take risks.

I often hear individuals remark, "What is the worst that could possibly happen to you. Will it kill you? However, death is hardly the worst possible outcome. Allowing yourself to die inside while still alive is the worst thing that can happen to you.

This tightrope walk between dwelling and remembering requires improved self-awareness. The longer you dwell on your mistakes, the more uncomfortable and hesitant you become, while forgetting them altogether makes you more likely to repeat them. The secret to balance resides in your capacity to translate setbacks into improvement nuggets. This generates the tendency to immediately stand back up after falling.

Mentally tough individuals welcome failure because they recognize that it paves the path to achievement. No one has ever achieved genuine success without first accepting defeat.

Your failures pave the route to success by indicating when you are on the incorrect path. Typically, the greatest breakthroughs occur when you are feeling the most irritated and trapped. This irritation encourages you to think differently, to think outside the box, and to recognize the solution you've been overlooking.

Mentally robust individuals are aware that where one focuses their attention impacts their emotional state. When you dwell on your difficulties, you generate and prolong unpleasant feelings and stress, which impairs your performance. When you concentrate on improving yourself and your surroundings, you develop a sense of personal efficacy, which generates pleasant emotions and enhances performance.

Mentally robust individuals remove themselves from their errors without forgetting them. By putting their past errors at a safe distance, yet still within reach, individuals are able to adapt and modify for future success.

When you derive your sense of pleasure and satisfaction from comparing yourself to others, you are no longer in control of your own happiness. When mentally strong people feel good about anything they do, they will not allow the opinions or achievements of others to diminish that feeling.

While it is hard to turn off your reactions to what others think of you, you do not have to compare yourself to others, and you can always take the opinions of others with a grain of salt. Mentally tough individuals are aware that regardless of what others think of them at any given moment, one thing is certain: they are never as good or horrible as they are seen to be.

Mentally tough individuals do not pass judgment on others because they recognize that everyone has something to offer and they do not need to put others down in order to feel better about themselves.

Comparing oneself to others is restrictive. Jealousy and anger sap your vitality; they are enormous energy drains. Mentally robust individuals do not waste time or energy evaluating others and fretting about whether they measure up.

Instead of wasting your focus on envy, channel your energy into gratitude. When you applaud the accomplishments of others, you and they both benefit.

According to a study conducted at the Eastern Ontario Research Institute, participants who exercised twice per week for ten weeks felt more socially, academically, and athletically competent. Additionally, they assessed their body image and self-esteem as greater. Best of all, rather than the physical changes in their bodies being responsible for the confidence boost, which is essential for mental toughness, it was the immediate endorphin-fueled happiness from exercise that made all the difference.

It is difficult to overemphasize the significance of sleep for enhancing mental resilience. During sleep, the brain eliminates harmful proteins, which are byproducts of waking neuronal activity. Unfortunately, your brain can remove them effectively only while you're asleep, so when you don't get enough sleep, the poisonous proteins remain in your brain cells, wreaking havoc by reducing your capacity to think, which caffeine cannot solve.

Mentally robust individuals are aware that sleep deprivation impairs their self-control, concentration, and memory, therefore they make quality sleep a top priority.

Caffeine stimulates the release of adrenaline, the hormone responsible for the fight-or-flight response, when consumed in excess. The fight-or-flight response bypasses rational thought in favor of a quicker reaction to ensure survival. This is advantageous when a bear is after you, but less so when life throws you a curveball.

When coffee induces this hyperarousal state of stress in your brain and body, your emotions control your conduct. The prolonged half-life of caffeine assures that you will remain alert as it takes its sweet time to leave the body. Mentally robust individuals are aware that too much caffeine is problematic, and they do not allow it to affect them.

Mentally robust individuals are aware that life goes much more smoothly after letting go of grudges and forgiving even those who never apologize. Grudges allow unfavorable occurrences from the past to destroy enjoyment in the present. Hatred and rage are emotional parasites that eat away at your happiness in life.

The negative feelings associated with harboring a grudge produce a stress reaction in the body, and harboring stress can have devastating effects both physically and mentally.
When you forgive someone, it does not mean that you condone their acts; rather, it means that you are no longer their victim.

Observe the news for any length of time, and you will notice that war, violent attacks, weak economies, failing enterprises, and environmental calamities form an ongoing cycle. It is simple to believe that the world is rapidly deteriorating.

And who can say! Perhaps it is. Mentally robust individuals, however, are unconcerned because they do not get caught up in things they cannot control. Instead of attempting to create a revolution overnight, they devote their energy into the two things wholly within their control: their attention and their effort.

Mental toughness is not an innate trait possessed by a chosen few. It is attainable and enjoyable.

Intentionally left blank

CHAPTER FOUR
How to Develop Mental Toughness: 14 Ways to Improve Your Mental Strength

While some people appear to be able to rapidly recover from personal mistakes and setbacks, others appear to have a considerably more difficult time doing so.

When you are knocked down by life, how quickly are you able to pull yourself up and adjust to the new circumstances? Or do you frequently feel helpless and utterly defeated by the scope and complexity of the problem, with little faith that you can discover a solution.

If you find that you fall into the second category, there is no need for alarm. It is a quality that can be developed and perfected through experience, self-discipline, and diligent effort, which is fortunate because there are a number of concrete ways for constructing mental resilience.

When unanticipated and unfavorable changes occur in our lives, like the passing of a loved one, the termination of a romantic relationship, or the loss of a job, our capacity for resilience is frequently put to the test. However, when faced with obstacles of this nature, you have the opportunity to rise above them and emerge from the experience even stronger than you were before.

Continue reading to acquire skills that can help you construct and strengthen your mental resilience, enabling you to more successfully deal with the problems that life throws at you.

How to Develop a Robust Mental Attitude

The capacity of an individual to deal productively with stressors, pressures, and obstacles and to perform to the best of their abilities, regardless of the circumstances in which they find themselves, is referred to as mental strength.

Developing your mental toughness is one of the most important aspects of living your greatest life. In the same way that we go to the gym and lift weights in order to improve our skeletal muscles, we must also cultivate our mental health by making use of various mental tools and strategies.

Having our mental health in top shape enables us to live a life that we enjoy, have meaningful connections with other people, and have healthy self-esteem. In addition to this, it helps us become more comfortable taking chances, expanding our horizons, and overcoming challenges that life inevitably brings our way.

Adopting mental toughness requires developing regular practices that work to create mental muscle. It also requires breaking the habits that are holding you back and bringing you down.

In order to be mentally healthy, we must build up our mental strength! Mental strength is something that is built through time by those who choose to make personal development a priority. Much like witnessing physical advantages from working out and eating properly, we must create healthy mental habits, like practicing appreciation, if we want to experience mental health gains.

Likewise, to experience physical advantages we must also give up bad behaviors, such as consuming junk food, and for mental gains, give up unhealthy habits such as feeling sorry for oneself.

We are all able to get intellectually stronger, the trick is to continuously practise and train your mental muscles just as you would if you were attempting to acquire physical strength!

Building Resilience and Mental Toughness

The term "Resilience," often used in reference to positive mental health, is really drawn from engineering, where it refers to the ability of a substance or item to spring back into shape. In the same way that a material thing would require strength and flexibility in order to bounce back, so too does a human require these attributes in order to be mentally resilient.

Mental resilience is defined by the American Psychological Association as:

"the ability to recover quickly from or adapt positively to adverse conditions," including "adversity," "trauma," "tragedy," "threats," and "severe stress."

A comparable idea, Mental Toughness, relates to the ability to stay strong in the face of adversity; to keep your focus and resolve despite the hardships you confront. A mentally tough individual sees challenge and adversity as an opportunity and not a threat, and has the confidence and positive outlook to accept what comes in their stride.

To be mentally tough, you must have some degree of resilience, but not all resilient persons are necessarily mentally tough. If you think of it as a metaphor, resilience would be the mountain, while mental toughness may be one of the tactics for ascending that mountain.

Strycharczyk (2015) finds it instructive to conceive of the difference in terms of the phrase 'survive and prosper.' Resilience helps you to survive, and mental toughness helps you to succeed.

Mental toughness begins when you choose to take attention of what's flowing through your mind, without identifying personally with those thoughts or sensations. Then, finding the determination to generate happy ideas regarding the issue at hand.

According to Strycharczyk and Cloughe, strategies for increasing mental toughness revolve around five themes:

Positive Thinking
Anxiety Control
Visualization
Control of One's Attention and Goal-Setting
In the same way that gaining mental strength requires self-awareness and commitment, increasing mental toughness also requires these things. In general, it seems as though individuals who are mentally tough achieve more than those who are mentally sensitive and have a higher level of contentment in their lives.

Control, commitment, confidence, and challenge are the four important characteristics of mental toughness that are described by Turner (2017). He refers to these characteristics as the 4Cs. It's possible to have some of these characteristics, but having all four of them together is what really sets successful people apart.

The MTQ48 Psychometric Tool, which was developed by Professor Peter Clough of Manchester Metropolitan University, is one method that can be used to assess an individual's mental toughness. The MTQ48 Tool is founded on this 4C's framework, which measures important aspects of mental toughness. As a result, it possesses both scientific validity and reliability.

The following are the four "C's" of mental toughness: (Turner, 2017)
1. Control
This refers to the degree to which you believe that you are in command of your life, including your feelings and your perception of the meaning of your existence. Your sense of pride in yourself is one way to think of the control aspect. A high score on the control scale indicates that an individual is confident

in their own skin and possesses a strong awareness of their own identity.

You are able to exercise self-control over your feelings, making it less likely that others will learn about your emotional condition, and you are also less prone to be sidetracked by the feelings of others. A low score on the control scale indicates that a person may have the perception that things just "happen to them" and that they have little or no control or influence over the course of their lives.

2. Dedicated service

This demonstrates the level of personal focus and reliability you possess. For someone to have a high level of commitment, they must be able to properly set goals and consistently fulfill them, without becoming distracted by other things. If you have a high level of commitment, it means that you are good at developing routines and habits that lead to increased levels of achievement.

If you have a low score on the commitment scale, it implies that you may have difficulty setting and prioritizing goals, as well as developing routines or habits that are indicative of success. There's also a possibility that you're easily distracted by other individuals or conflicting priorities.

The Resilience component of the definition of Mental Toughness can be represented by the Control and Commitment scales when taken together. This makes perfect sense when you consider that being able to recover quickly from adversity demands a strong sense that you are in command of your life and have the ability to make adjustments. In addition to this, it demands concentration as well as the capacity to create routines and goals that will help you go back on the route you originally picked.

3. Challenge

This demonstrates the degree to which you are self-motivated and flexible. If you have a high score on the Challenge scale, it indicates that you are highly motivated to perform at your personal best, that you view difficulties, change, and adversity as opportunities rather than threats, and that you are likely to be adaptable and nimble. If you have a low score on the challenge scale, it indicates that you may view change as a threat and shy away from unusual or trying situations because you are afraid of failing.

4. Confidence

This is the amount to which you believe in your abilities to be productive and capable; this is both your belief in yourself and the idea that you can influence other people. To have a high level of confidence means that you feel that you will be able to successfully complete tasks, that you can shrug off failures while still maintaining your routine, and that you can even get stronger in your determination. To have a poor ranking on the

If you score low on the confidence scale, it indicates that you are easily unsettled by setbacks and that you do not believe that you are capable of anything or that you have any influence over others.

The Confidence component of the concept of Mental Toughness is represented by the combined scores of the Challenge and Confidence scales. This exemplifies a person's capacity to recognize and seize possibilities, as well as their awareness of circumstances as opportunities to embrace and investigate. This makes perfect sense when you consider that the likelihood of overcoming obstacles and achieving one's goals is directly proportional to one's level of self-assurance in both oneself and one's capabilities, as well as the ease with which one interacts with others.

How to Build Resilience in Adults

As said before, mental resilience is not a trait that people either have or don't have. Rather, it involves habits, attitudes, and actions that may be learnt and developed in everyone. Of course, there may be a hereditary component to a person's amount of mental resilience, but it is clearly something that can be worked upon.

Southwick, Bonanno, Masten, Panter-Brick, and Yehuda (2013) wrote a paper that sought to answer some of the most pressing questions in the field of resilience research, and they were inspired to do so by a panel presented at the 2013 conference of the International Society for Traumatic Stress Studies.

The panelists had slightly diverse definitions of resilience, but most of the concepts incorporated a sense of healthy, adaptive, good functioning in the aftermath of hardship. They all agreed that "resilience is a complex idea that can be understood in different ways by different people, families, organizations, civilizations, and cultures."

There was also a consensus that one's potential to develop resilience is reliant on various factors, including genetic, developmental, demographic, cultural, economic, and social variables; but that resilience can be built, nonetheless (Southwick et al., 2013).

Simply put, resilience may be fostered through will-power, discipline, and hard effort; and there are several techniques through which to do so. The goal is to identify strategies that are likely to work effectively for you as part of your own specific plan for fostering resilience.

Increase Mental Strength in Students

Just like adults, mentally robust children and adolescents are able to confront issues, bounce back from failure, and cope with life's obstacles and tribulations. They are resilient and have the fortitude and confidence to attain their greatest potential.

Growing mental strength in students is just as vital, if not more important, as developing mental power in adults, helping kids develop mental strength involves a three-pronged strategy, teaching them how to:

Replace negative thinking with good, more realistic thoughts.
They need to learn to master their feelings so that their feelings won't master them.
Act in a constructive manner.
Even though there are a great number of strategies, methods of discipline, and teaching tools that assist children in developing their mental muscle, the following ten strategies are some of the most effective in assisting students in developing the strength they will need to become mentally strong adults:

- Instruct Individualized Abilities

Instead of making children suffer as a result of their own failures, the focus of discipline should be on instructing children on how to perform better the next time. Use consequences that teach valuable skills such as problem-solving and impulse control rather than punishments to correct undesirable behaviors.

- Allow Your Child to Learn from Their Mistakes

Making mistakes is a natural and necessary aspect of both life and the learning process. Teach your child or one of your students that this is true and that they have no reason to feel embarrassed or ashamed about making a mistake in their work.

- Show your kid how to have positive conversations with themselves.

It is crucial to teach youngsters how to build a perspective on life that is both realistic and hopeful, as well as how to reframe negative thoughts when they do occur. They will be better able to persevere through challenging situations if they acquire this ability at a young age.

- Encouraging Your Child to Confront Their Fears Head-On

Giving your child the opportunity to confront their fears head-on will help them gain confidence that will serve them well throughout their lives. Your child can learn to overcome their fears by facing them one small step at a time and stepping outside of their comfort zone, while you praise and reward their efforts. This is one way to accomplish this goal.

- Permit Your Child to Experience Uncomfortable Feelings

It is important to allow them to sometimes lose or struggle, and to insist that they are responsible even when they do not want to be. It can be tempting to try to comfort or rescue your child or student whenever they are having difficulty, but it is important to resist the temptation. Children's mental resilience can be improved by giving them opportunities to face and overcome challenges on their own.

- Develop Your Personality

Children will have a stronger ability to make good decisions about their health if they have a robust moral compass and value system. You can be of assistance by imparting principles like honesty and compassion, as well as by regularly creating learning experiences that serve to reinforce such qualities.

- Make Having Gratitude Your Number One
  Priority

Having a grateful attitude and showing that attitude
to others is one of the best things you can do for
your mental health, and the same is true for children.
Even in the most trying of circumstances, the
practice of gratitude enables us to keep things in
proper perspective. You may help your child
develop a healthy mind by instilling a sense of
thankfulness in them and encouraging them to
express it on a regular basis.

- Recognize and Accept Your Own Personal
  Responsibility

In order to acquire mental strength, it is necessary to
acknowledge and accept responsibility for one's own
acts and faults. If you notice that one of your
students is attempting to place blame on other
people for his or her own thoughts, feelings, or
actions, you should simply guide them away from
excuses and toward explanations.

- Instruct Students in the Art of Emotional
  Self-Regulation

Instead of trying to soothe or calm down your child
every time they are upset, teach them how to deal

with uncomfortable emotions on their own so that they do not grow up dependent on you to regulate their mood. This will prevent them from becoming emotionally dependent on you as they get older. Children are better equipped to handle the ups and downs of life if they have an understanding of the spectrum of their own feelings.

- Set an Example for Mental Toughness by Being a Role Model

There is no more effective method of education than leading by example with a child. You have to set an example for your kids or children by being mentally strong yourself if you want them to follow in your footsteps. Demonstrate to them that you place a high importance on personal development in your life and have a conversation with them about the objectives you have set for yourself and the efforts you take to develop your skills.

How to Develop Mental Toughness and Stay Strong

Are you the kind of person who dreams of having an incredible amount of success in their lives? Have you trained your mind to be resilient enough to pull that off.

The pursuit of success, no matter how lofty your goals may be, can be challenging, and the monotony of day-to-day life can sap your strength on multiple levels over time, including the physical, the mental, and the emotional. I think we can all agree on this point.

On the road to achievement and high performance, people from all walks of life and circumstances encounter a variety of challenges, including but not limited to: failure, burnout, discouragement, tiredness, limiting beliefs about themselves, stress, and so on.

Why do some people remain committed to working toward their own goals year after year, while others simply give up? How are those individuals able to maintain their strength and continue when the odds are so overwhelmingly stacked against them.

Recent research has demonstrated that having a strong mental capacity is an essential component of success. Grit is a book written by Angela Duckworth that you should read if you haven't already. In it, she demonstrates that "the secret to extraordinary performance is not talent but a specific balance of passion and tenacity she calls 'grit'." Grit is her term for the combination of passion and determination. To put it another way, having a mentally strong disposition is essential when it comes to accomplishing one's goals.

When it comes down to its most basic definition, mental toughness may be summed up as the capacity to persevere in the face of adversity. Others who have higher levels of mental toughness are able to overcome these challenges and pave the way for future success, whereas those who have lower levels of mental toughness may give up on their goals and aspirations.

The good news is that regardless of who you are, what others have told you, or what you currently believe, you have the ability to cultivate the mental toughness that is necessary for you to be successful.

- Cultivate a more optimistic outlook on life

If you want to be able to handle stress better and have a higher mental toughness, the first thing you need to do is make it a priority to cultivate a powerful and optimistic mentality in your day-to-day life.

According to research conducted at the Cleveland Clinic, the typical person experiences 60,000 thoughts in a single day. Ninety-five percent of those thoughts are repeated every single day, and the majority of the time, eighty percent of those repeated concepts are negative.

That's approximately 45,600 unfavorable thoughts every single day.

Keeping these unfavorable ideas in your head is comparable to going on a walk in the mountains while carrying a load full of boulders. The hike is challenging enough on its own, but adding extra baggage that slows you down and makes it harder to move is a surefire way to fail.

When it comes to developing mental toughness, there are times when the focus should be less on gaining new strength and more on conserving your existing strength for the activities that require it. Instead of trying to get strong enough to handle the additional weight, wouldn't it be easier to drop the pebbles out of the backpack instead of trying to do so?

- Let Go of Limiting Beliefs About Yourself
When you repeatedly criticize and berate yourself, it's not exactly the best way to build mental toughness. Beliefs that are self-limiting are any beliefs that prevent you from moving forward in some way.

When we let these self-limiting beliefs free reign in our minds, negative self-talk takes over, and we find it increasingly difficult to think in a constructive manner as a result.

When you become aware that you are entertaining a self-limiting notion, you should swiftly put an end to it by convincing yourself that it is not true, and then you should back up that assertion with some positive affirmations:

I am intelligent enough; yet, it is possible that I need to perform some additional research beforehand.

It's possible that I don't have as much experience as someone else, but it won't prevent me from giving it a shot. My prior work experience is sufficient for me to begin. I'll figure out how to do the rest as I go along."

"Just because I was unsuccessful the prior time does not indicate I will be unsuccessful this time. My past does not influence my future."

Put an end to thinking in terms of either all or nothing.

All-or-nothing thinking is another type of negative thinking that could be getting in the way of your progress toward developing mental toughness.

Thinking in extremes is what is meant by the concept of all-or-nothing thinking. You are either a winner or a loser in your endeavor. Your performance was either very good or very poor. If you are not flawless, then you are not worthy of success.

However, this is not the case!

If you set out to drop 30 pounds but only managed to shed 28 instead, wouldn't you consider that a success even though it wasn't as much as you had hoped? I'd say so!

If you let an all-or-nothing way of thinking take control of your head, you will feel like you're on cloud nine when you succeed, but you will be extremely hard on yourself when you "fail." You will be able to experience success more frequently if you are willing to acknowledge the nuances that exist between black and white.

When you become aware that you are having an all-or-nothing thought, it is important to remind yourself to seek for the good aspects of the circumstance. What did you gain by trying? What opportunities or experiences could you not have had if you had not taken a risk? If you gave it another shot, do you think you could do better?

Dwelling on the negative is harmful to mental health and should be avoided at all costs. Self-limiting beliefs and all-or-nothing thinking are two factors that can contribute to this mental health problem. You have to get out of the house if you want to cultivate some mental toughness and maintain a healthy mind.

When we ruminate on our misfortunes, we squander a significant quantity of energy that we may be putting toward working toward our objectives instead. When something like this occurs, our likelihood of quitting completely increases.

That doesn't mean you don't have a tough mind; it just means you're not making the most of the energy you have.

When something negative happens in the future, it is vital to let yourself feel the sadness and frustration that you are feeling, but you should also make an effort to decrease the amount of time that you spend dwelling on the problem.

If you find that you are having difficulty with this, you might want to try the following:

Make a phone call to a trusted friend or advisor and discuss the situation with them. Get some outside insight on your problem.

Your ability to dwell is restricted by time, and you can do so for no more than sixty minutes at a time. The next step is to motivate yourself to go on by reminding yourself that you are a human being and that it is okay for you to make errors and suffer from setbacks.

If everything else fails, come up with a productive strategy to divert your attention so that you may collect your thoughts and reassess the situation with a level head.

The sooner you are able to shift your attention to the positive aspects of the situation and put it in the past, the sooner you will be able to resume working toward your life goals of obtaining success.

- Reconcile yourself with your life's mission. Having a compelling "why" for each of your short-term and long-term goals is one of the most important aspects of developing mental toughness and maintaining a robust and focused mind.

If you don't have a compelling reason "why" you want to achieve a significant objective, you're much more likely to become sidetracked, disheartened, or disengaged as soon as you encounter your first obstacle on the path to achieving that goal.

Consider the most recent instance in which you were attempting to work toward a goal or resolution, but things weren't going as planned. You might have believed that you lacked the necessary amount of self-control or determination.

It is more likely that you simply did not have a rationale that was compelling enough.

Around the world, people are hearing the message that "Start with Why" author Simon Sinek has been spreading. In essence, he is arguing that:

"Your 'why' is the reason, the cause, or the concept that motivates you."

Pursuing a goal or doing an activity for which you do not have a compelling reason to do so is one of the most significant ways in which your mental energy can be depleted. Quite frequently, we make goals not because we want to achieve them in practice but because we like the concept of the goal. Without establishing a connection to our reasons for doing something, we are unable to inherently inspire ourselves to accomplish even our most difficult objectives.

- Find your own internal drive.

Intrinsic motivation is our natural desire to do something. It happens when we work toward something that makes us happy more than anything else, not our parents, bosses, or teachers.

Use intrinsic motivation to build mental toughness Let's say you think you want to stop smoking because you know it's bad for you, but you really like smoking. No matter how strong your willpower or how tough your mind is, you won't be able to quit smoking if you don't really want to.

But if you want to quit smoking because you just had a baby and you don't want your child to grow up around smoke, that "why" will give you intrinsic motivation. Intrinsic motivation is much more powerful than just being stubborn, and it's also much easier to keep up over time.

If you're trying to build mental toughness, putting a "why" behind everything you want to do will make it easier and take less effort to do those things.

- Find Strength in Being Together

The last step in building mental toughness is to realize that you're not in this by yourself.

Bill Gates did not make Microsoft all by himself. Oprah's network wasn't built by her alone. Steve Jobs didn't come up with the iPhone on his own. The "Let's Move" campaign wasn't started by Michelle Obama on her own.

Behind all of these successful people were a lot of other people who helped them, gave them advice, and gave them support.

If you want to build mental toughness that can't be beat, you need to know that you don't have to do everything by yourself. Even the toughest Navy Seals have a group of people who help them.

Find a guide or a group of guides.

There are too many benefits of having a good mentor to list them all, but in a nutshell, a mentor is someone who helps you find your greatest strengths, see and get past your blind spots, and work through your weaknesses.

If you're having trouble dealing with your own negative thoughts or figuring out what you want to do with your life, talk to a mentor about it. A mentor can help us step back and see the bigger picture when we get too caught up in the details.

Here's how you can find the best mentor for you: How to Look for a Mentor Who Can Help You Succeed

- Recruit Some Cheerleaders

If you want to stay strong, it doesn't hurt to have a group of people cheering you on and helping you reach your goals. A group of cheerleaders will help keep your spirits up, unlike mentors who will jump in and help you solve your problems.

Even if you have a strong "why" and a positive outlook, it's almost impossible to always have a good attitude. It doesn't mean you're weak if you sometimes need help. It makes a huge difference to have a group of people cheering you on.

Tell a few close friends what you're doing to reach your goals, and let them know when things get hard.

When they give you the pep talk you need, don't fight against their positive words or try to counter them with your own negative thoughts.

Let their hope fill you up, and then use that energy to keep going.

- Establish a Group for Responsibility. Although cheerleaders are wonderful, there are times when we need that extra push from someone else in order to keep going. You may have a compelling reason for wanting to run a marathon or lose 30 pounds, but that doesn't mean it's going to be easy. Trying to force yourself to follow through is a sure way to tax your mental energy, so make sure you have a good reason for doing whatever it is you want to do before you start.

Rather than wasting part of the mental energy you have, why not join a group that will hold you accountable?

Look for an individual or a group of people who have objectives that are comparable to yours, or at the very least, the requirement of an accountability partner. The next step is to reach a consensus among the members of the group on the necessity of daily competition.

- **Acquire the Capacity to Get Back Up After Falling Down**

It's not a piece of cake to cultivate a resilient mindset and toughen up your mental game! You are not any different from anyone else who has ever achieved a significant amount of success in that you will undoubtedly face challenges, experience setbacks, and experience failure.

You are likely to experience a lot of highs and lows while you work toward achieving your goals; nevertheless, this does not indicate that you lack mental toughness, willpower, or discipline.

Instead of giving up immediately when you find yourself in a difficult situation, try asking yourself the following questions:

Shouldn't I be a little easier on myself?
Am I allowing my negative thoughts to cloud my judgment?

What could have been done differently to avoid this failure?
Why was it so vital for me to achieve this goal?
What exactly was the point of me?
Does achieving this objective still hold value for me?
Whom could I approach for assistance? Who can act as a role model for me or keep me accountable?

It is a terrific method to check in on your thinking to ask yourself these questions every once in a while. It is far too simple for us to become disheartened when we allow ourselves to become consumed by negative thoughts or when we lose connection to our mission.

- Bringing Everything Together

Learning to recognize negative tendencies and taking proactive steps to remedy them early on through the development of good habits is an essential component of developing mental toughness. Building up your mental toughness does not involve getting rid of your weaknesses, but rather learning how to cope with and triumph over them.

No one is flawless, but if we direct our attention to the appropriate things, we may develop a mental toughness that is equal to the greatest tests that life can throw at us.

Why is it so Difficult to Achieve Mental Strength?

Your mind is a very potent instrument. It has the potential to be either your greatest ally or your gravest foe. The catch is that everyone has that voice inside their head, also known as their inner critic. Here's the thing, though: we all have it.

This voice does not have any compassion for you; instead, it takes pleasure in putting you down and working to persuade you that you are not the leader of your own life.

You do not have adequate physical strength.

You have some serious issues.

You are not deserving of joy in your life.

Fortuitously, a significant number of people let this voice dull their light and control every decision they make in their life. Your inner critic, in a nutshell, saps your mental fortitude and undermines your self-confidence. Nevertheless, it is essential that we do not stifle this voice without first gaining an awareness of its origin.

A significant number of individuals make the mistake of believing that just because they are thinking negative thoughts about themselves, that these thoughts must be accurate. Wrong.

In reality, your inner critic is just your inner child acting out. Psychologists think these voices are leftovers from traumatic events that occurred in childhood. We eventually become so accustomed to living under these narratives that we fail to recognize them or call them into question.

Ironically, your inner critic is actually trying to be of assistance to you. That is the epitome of playing tricks on one's mind! I would like to put up an alternative viewpoint. What if, rather than engaging in a battle with this critical voice, you tried to redefine the intention that was driving it.

You can be of assistance to yourself by reframing your inner critic as your inner coach.

A critic will bring you down, but a coach will push you to find answers to problems and give you the confidence to confront new difficulties with grace, courage, and persistence.

You may, for instance, say the following aloud to yourself: "Critic, thank you for trying so hard to keep me safe, but at this point, it's time for you to move aside now."

The amazing thing about life is that at any point in time, you have the ability to rewrite your story and release the strength that has always been a part of you. This is one of the most beautiful aspects of life.

I want you to imagine that your mind is a muscle that you can exercise. You have to make the same kind of commitment to flexing your mental muscle as you do to going to the gym and working on building up your physical strength.

At the end of the day, achieving success is largely a game of mindset. As Tony Robbins says,

"Only twenty percent of success is related to strategy, which comprises the exact procedures necessary to attain a result. Eighty percent of achievement is related to psychology, which encompasses a person's thinking, attitudes, and emotions."

CONCLUSION

How do you pick yourself up after being knocked down by life and left feeling battered and bruised? What are some things you can do to help yourself get back in the game? It is only normal to react by becoming increasingly anxious and panicked. A knockout can be intellectually and emotionally draining, and let's face it, that's just the way it is.

Mental toughness, in my view, is the single most important factor separating people who are able to prosper in life from those who crumble at the first sight of difficulty in their journey through this world.

Mental strength is the capacity of an individual to persevere in the face of adversity and emerge victorious as a result of their efforts . It is the magic ingredient that enables you to power through fatigue even when every fiber in your body is screaming at you to give up. Discover how to draw on the mental fortitude you already possess in order to make progress.

Self-awareness and acceptance serve as the foundation for a number of the techniques and strategies listed here that might help you improve your mental health. In order to enhance, improve, or build upon our existing mental strength, we need to first be aware of where we are and then accept that this is where we are. Only then can we enhance, improve, or build upon our existing mental capacity. Not until then will we be able to take the first baby steps toward a more robust and healthy mental state.

You are not in control of everything that takes place to you, but you are in complete command of how you respond to the events that take place. In circumstances like these, your mind has the potential to be either your greatest tool or your worst enemy. You will be able to recover quickly from challenging circumstances and be capable of extraordinary achievements if you learn how to train it correctly.

If you want to be more content with your life as a whole, maintaining a healthy mental state is really necessary. Strength, toughness, and resilience are all important components of mental fitness. Building these muscles may be very difficult and may take years of effort and commitment, but the benefits of being mentally fit and resilient will be seen in all aspects of your life. Building these muscles may take years of effort and commitment.

The development of healthy mental habits and the abandonment of poor mental habits can lead to improvements in performance, as well as in one's relationships and overall sense of well-being.

By putting these tactics into practice and committing to the process over the long term, each of us has the ability to enhance our mental health.

Make today the first day of your journey to improve your mental toughness.

Your mental fortitude is greater than any challenge or difficulty you may face. You have the option of remaining on the ground and playing the role of the victim, or you may choose to raise yourself up and turn your suffering into opportunity.

Printed in Great Britain
by Amazon

26429590R00076